Contents

The Effects of Potential Cuts in SNAP Spending on Households With Different Amounts of Income

Summary

The Supplemental Nutrition Assistance Program (SNAP, formerly known as Food Stamps) provides benefits to low-income households to help them buy food. Total federal expenditures on SNAP amounted to $76 billion in fiscal year 2014. In an average month that year, 47 million people (or one in seven U.S. residents) received SNAP benefits.

Some policymakers have expressed a desire to scale back the program significantly to reduce federal spending. In this report, the Congressional Budget Office examines several options for doing so and their effects on the benefits that would be received by households with different amounts of income.

Who Receives SNAP Benefits?

Most people receiving SNAP benefits live in households with very low income, and SNAP benefits represent a significant supplement to their income. In fiscal year 2013, about 85 percent of households receiving benefits had monthly income (excluding SNAP benefits) below the federal poverty guidelines. (Those guidelines are commonly known as the federal poverty level, or FPL; for a household of three, the FPL in 2015 is about $1,700 per month, or about $20,000 per year.) SNAP benefits boosted monthly income for participating households by 36 percent, on average, in 2013.[1]

A household's SNAP benefits are calculated according to its income and size. The maximum benefit for a household of three in the contiguous United States is currently $511 per month, or about $5.60 per person per day. However, if a household's income (minus allowable deductions, such as those for housing expenses) increases, each additional dollar in income reduces SNAP benefits by 30 cents—until its income reaches a certain threshold, at which point benefits are stopped altogether.

How Would Reducing SNAP Benefits Affect Households' Income?

CBO examined what would happen to households' income if spending on SNAP in 2016—which CBO currently projects to be about $77 billion—was cut by 15 percent.[2] Such a decline would save $11.5 billion in 2016, putting inflation-adjusted spending roughly on par with spending in 2009. Specifically, CBO examined three illustrative options, each of which would cut federal spending on SNAP in 2016 by 15 percent:

■ Reducing SNAP benefits for all participants by reducing the maximum benefit by 13 percent and leaving other program rules unchanged (which would result in benefit cuts for all beneficiaries);

■ Increasing the rate at which benefits decline from the maximum benefit, as a household's income (minus allowable deductions) increases, from 30 percent of the additional income to 49 percent; and

---

1. Kelsey Farson Gray, *Characteristics of Supplemental Nutrition Assistance Program Households: Fiscal Year 2013*, SNAP-14-CHAR (submitted by Mathematica Policy Research to the Department of Agriculture, Food and Nutrition Service, Office of Policy Support, December 2014), http://go.usa.gov/3aKHP.

2. Although CBO's baseline projections and cost estimates are reported for fiscal years, which run from October 1 to September 30 and are designated by the calendar year in which they end, this report focuses on changes in benefits paid to households and other income received by those households during the calendar year. Total spending on SNAP is projected to be $77.3 billion in fiscal year 2016 and $76.0 billion in fiscal year 2017.

- Reducing the monthly income limit for eligibility from 130 percent to 67 percent of the FPL, while maintaining benefit amounts for those who remain eligible (including households with elderly or disabled members and households eligible because they receive cash assistance from certain other programs).

Because very few households with higher annual income receive SNAP benefits under current law, the options would primarily affect households whose income was relatively low. However, groups of lower-income households would be affected differently, depending on how many in each group received SNAP benefits and the income of households in the group. To show those effects, CBO grouped households into deciles (that is, 10 percent shares of the population) according to their annual after-tax cash income (which excludes SNAP benefits); in 2016, CBO estimates, three-person households in the lowest decile will have annual after-tax cash income below about $15,000, those in the second decile will have income between about $15,000 and $25,000, and those in the third decile will have income between about $25,000 and $32,000.

Among the effects of the options that CBO estimates are the following:

- For households with annual after-tax cash income in the lowest decile of the income distribution in 2016, the first option would reduce income (including SNAP benefits) in that year by about $300, or about 4 percent, on average. That calculation includes not only households that would receive SNAP benefits under current law but also those that would not (and thus would experience no decline in income under the option). For households in the lowest income decile that would receive SNAP benefits under current law, the average decline in benefits would be about $600 per year. The other options would have significantly smaller effects on households in the lowest decile of income.

- For households with annual after-tax cash income in the second decile of the income distribution, each of the three options would reduce income in 2016 by about $250 to $500, or about 1 percent to 3 percent, on average; within that range, the first option would have the smallest effect, and the third would have the largest. Among households in that group that would receive SNAP benefits under current law, the average

decline in benefits under the three options would be between $550 and about $1,000 per year.

- For households with annual after-tax cash income in the third decile of the income distribution, the reduction in income from each of the three options in 2016 would range from about $100 to $200, or less than 1 percent, on average. Among households in that group that would receive SNAP benefits under current law, the average decline in benefits under the three options would be between $650 and $1,200 per year.

- Among all households in higher income deciles, the average effects of the options would be quite small. However, among households in those deciles that would receive SNAP benefits under current law, the average decline in benefits under the first option would be similar to the declines for the three lower income deciles. Under the second and third options, the decline in benefits for households in higher income deciles that would receive benefits under current law would be most similar to the decline experienced by households in the lowest income decile.

Some policymakers have suggested another option: converting SNAP into a block grant program for states. CBO has not analyzed the effects on different households' income of such an option, because those effects would depend on the amounts and conditions of the grants— and on decisions by state governments, which are very difficult to predict. However, under a block grant option that reduced federal spending on SNAP by 15 percent in 2016, *average* benefits would almost surely decline significantly unless state or private funding made up some or all of the difference.

CBO also assessed but did not quantify the effects of the options on SNAP recipients' incentives to work and consequently on households' labor income. Overall labor income would increase by a small amount under the first option, CBO expects, and decrease by a small amount under the second and third.

How SNAP Works

Although federal laws and regulations dictate the outlines of SNAP, states can select various policy options to modify the program. As a result, eligibility rules are not the same nationwide and can vary somewhat from the general principles presented below. Benefit calculations, however, are mostly the same nationwide, as is the maximum benefit that participants can receive.[3]

Eligibility

A household is generally eligible for SNAP if it participates in certain other assistance programs or if it can demonstrate that its income and assets are sufficiently small.[4] Lawfully present noncitizens must meet additional requirements to be eligible for SNAP, and unauthorized immigrants are ineligible. Most households do not face a limit on how long they may participate in SNAP, and most are not required to work to receive benefits.

Eligibility Through Participation in Other Programs.

Nine of every 10 households receiving SNAP benefits in fiscal year 2013 (the most recent year for which such data are available) were "categorically eligible"; that is, they qualified for those benefits in part because they participated in certain other federal or state programs. A quarter of the categorically eligible households qualified because all members received cash assistance from Temporary Assistance for Needy Families (TANF), Supplemental Security Income (SSI), or certain state programs serving people with low income. In the remaining three-quarters of the categorically eligible households, all members received or were authorized to receive noncash benefits from TANF—such as child care, transportation assistance, or even just a pamphlet describing TANF programs—and thereby qualified for SNAP benefits under "broad-based categorical eligibility."[5]

The vast majority of households that qualify for SNAP because of categorical eligibility (including broad-based categorical eligibility) would also meet the federal income and asset requirements for eligibility. In fact, many households that are categorically eligible for benefits are subject to income or asset tests, but those tests can be less stringent than the ones applied to households that are not categorically eligible.

Eligibility Through Income and Asset Tests.
Households that are not categorically eligible for SNAP—about 1 in 10 participating households in fiscal year 2013—can qualify if they meet certain monthly income and asset requirements, which are set by law and vary for households with different characteristics. For instance, households in which a member is at least 60 years old or disabled can generally qualify for SNAP with more income and assets than other qualifying households can have.

In general, households are subject to two income tests, one based on gross monthly income and the other on net monthly income. A household's gross income is its total cash income in the month when it applies for benefits. Net income is gross income minus allowable deductions, which include a standard deduction for all households and deductions based on the household's income and expenses (such as some housing and child care costs). Households can qualify for SNAP benefits if their gross income is no more than 130 percent, and if their net income is no more than 100 percent, of the monthly FPL.[6] For most areas of the country, the monthly FPL in fiscal year 2015 is $1,650 for a household of three and about $2,000 for a household of four; those amounts correspond to annual income of about $20,000 and $24,000, respectively. Households in which a member is at least 60 years old or disabled are not subject to the gross income test but are subject to the net income test.

Households are also subject to an asset test. In general, a household may have no more than $2,250 in assets of certain kinds to be eligible for SNAP; for a household with at least one person who is at least 60 years old or disabled, the asset limit is currently $3,250. Those amounts rise over time with inflation. The test counts cash, money in bank accounts, and other financial resources, but it does not count certain other assets that a household may own, such as a primary residence, a vehicle (in most states), or money in retirement or education savings accounts.

---

3. The maximum benefit is higher in some areas, such as Hawaii and Alaska. For more information on how SNAP works, see Congressional Budget Office, *The Supplemental Nutrition Assistance Program* (April 2012), www.cbo.gov/publication/43173.

4. SNAP benefits are awarded to so-called food assistance units, which are groups of people who live together—no family relationship is required—and share the purchase, preparation, and consumption of food. Food assistance units are generally equivalent to households and are referred to as households in this analysis.

5. Kelsey Farson Gray, *Characteristics of Supplemental Nutrition Assistance Program Households: Fiscal Year 2013*, SNAP-14-CHAR (submitted by Mathematica Policy Research to the Department of Agriculture, Food and Nutrition Service, Office of Policy Support, December 2014), http://go.usa.gov/3aKHP.

---

6. Those households generally have to recertify their eligibility every 6 or 12 months.

Table 1.

Characteristics of Households Receiving SNAP Benefits, Fiscal Year 2013

Households With	Number of Households (Millions)[a]	Share of Total (Percent)[a]	Average Gross Monthly Income (2013 Dollars)	Average Monthly SNAP Benefit (2013 Dollars)
Earnings	7.1	31	1,219	322
Supplemental Security Income	4.5	20	895	205
TANF Income	1.5	7	708	432
No Gross Income[b]	4.9	22	0	284
Children	10.2	45	971	410
People at Least 60 Years Old	4.0	17	883	134
Disabled People Younger Than 60	4.6	20	984	204
No Children, People at Least 60 Years Old, or Disabled People	5.7	25	256	195
All Households	**22.8**	**100**	**758**	**271**

Source: Congressional Budget Office based on Kelsey Farson Gray, *Characteristics of Supplemental Nutrition Assistance Program Households: Fiscal Year 2013* (submitted by Mathematica Policy Research to the Department of Agriculture, Food and Nutrition Service, Office of Policy Support, December 2014), http://go.usa.gov/3aKHP.

Note: SNAP = Supplemental Nutrition Assistance Program; TANF = Temporary Assistance for Needy Families.

a.   The sum of households does not match the total because a household can fall in more than one category. For example, a household could have both children and people at least 60 years old.

b.   Gross income includes most cash income (such as earnings, Social Security income, Supplemental Security Income, and TANF income) and excludes most noncash income and in-kind benefits. It is a measure of income used to determine eligibility for SNAP.

Benefits

SNAP benefits are calculated in the same way for all beneficiaries, regardless of how they became eligible for the program: according to a household's net income and size. An eligible household with no net income (that is, with no income after the allowable deductions are made) receives the maximum benefit, which is determined by the number of people in the household and the cost of the Thrifty Food Plan (TFP), a basket of foods selected by the Department of Agriculture that would provide a nutritious diet for a household of that size.[7] In fiscal year 2015, for example, the maximum monthly benefit for a household of three in the contiguous United States is $511, or about $5.60 per person per day. A household that has net income is expected to spend 30 percent of it on food, so its SNAP benefit is reduced from the maximum by that amount. For example, if a three-person

household's net monthly income was $1,000 in 2015, its monthly SNAP benefit would be $211—that is, $511 minus 30 percent of $1,000—or about $2.30 per person per day.

Restrictions limit the items that may be purchased with SNAP benefits. Prohibited items include food hot at the point of sale (for example, pizza sold by the slice), alcoholic beverages, cigarettes, vitamins, medicines, and any other nonfood items. SNAP benefits are not cash; they are provided through electronic benefit transfer cards, which resemble debit cards but cannot be used to withdraw SNAP benefits in cash from an automated teller machine.

Characteristics of SNAP Recipients

Most people receiving SNAP benefits live in households with very low income. In fiscal year 2013, about 85 percent of households receiving benefits had income (excluding SNAP benefits) below the FPL (which is about $20,000 per year for a household of three in 2015). About 20 percent of recipient households reported income from SSI, and 7 percent reported income from TANF (see Table 1).

---

7.   In 2013, about 40 percent of households receiving SNAP benefits had no net income. See Kelsey Farson Gray, *Characteristics of Supplemental Nutrition Assistance Program Households: Fiscal Year 2013*, SNAP-14-CHAR (submitted by Mathematica Policy Research to the Department of Agriculture, Food and Nutrition Service, Office of Policy Support, December 2014), p. 35, http://go.usa.gov/3aKHP.

Figure 1.

Projected SNAP Benefits as a Share of All Households' Income in 2016

SNAP benefits constitute a large share of income for households in the lowest decile but are less important for higher-income households.

Decile of Households' Income

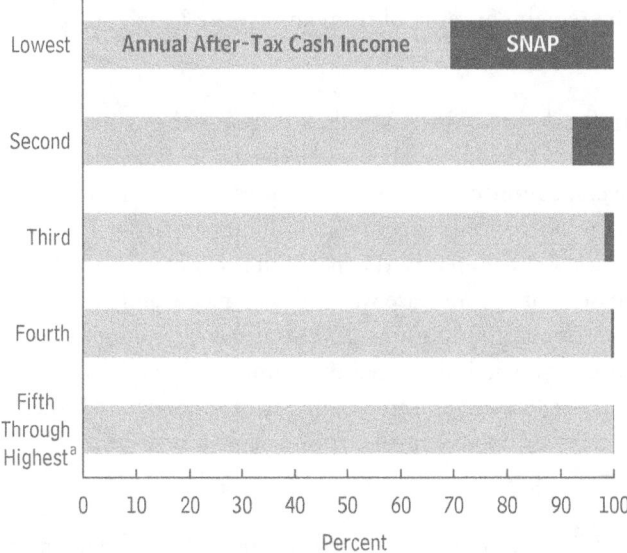

Source: Congressional Budget Office.

Notes: Benefits and income are shown for all households, including those that do not receive SNAP benefits.

CBO placed households into 10 income groups of equal size, or deciles, on the basis of their annual after-tax cash income, which excludes SNAP benefits and was adjusted for household size by dividing income by the FPL. After-tax cash income consists of market income and cash transfers, net of federal taxes paid or refundable tax credits received.

In 2016, CBO estimates, three-person households in the lowest decile of the income distribution will have annual after-tax cash income below about $15,000, those in the second decile will have income between about $15,000 and $25,000, and those in the third decile will have income between about $25,000 and $32,000.

FPL = federal poverty level (officially called the federal poverty guidelines); SNAP = Supplemental Nutrition Assistance Program.

a.   SNAP benefits are projected to constitute less than 0.05 percent of these households' income.

In fiscal year 2013, the most recent year for which detailed demographic data are available, about half of all households receiving SNAP benefits were single-person households, though some were much larger. On average, 2.1 people lived in each household. About 75 percent

of households receiving benefits included a child, a person at least 60 years old, or a disabled person younger than 60.[8]

Of the households that are eligible for SNAP, the poorer ones are likelier to participate than the less poor. About 85 percent of people estimated to be eligible for benefits received them in 2012 (the most recent year for which those data are available), but a much greater percentage, an estimated 96 percent, of the benefits that all eligible people could have received were paid out—which indicates that households receiving larger benefits, and therefore with less non-SNAP income, were participating in SNAP more than households with higher income were.[9]

The Effects of SNAP on Recipients

SNAP benefits represent a significant supplement to income for many low-income households. In 2016, those benefits are projected to constitute about 30 percent of income for all households in the bottom 10 percent of the distribution of annual after-tax cash income, on average—including those households that will not receive SNAP benefits at all (see Figure 1).[10] Benefits will be a smaller share of income for the average household with higher income.

In 2013, for households that participated in the program, SNAP benefits boosted monthly income by 36 percent, on average; the average increases for households with and without children were 42 percent and 27 percent, respectively. The average household receiving SNAP benefits in 2013 had an income (excluding SNAP benefits) of $758 per month in 2013 dollars, or about $9,100 per year. The monthly SNAP benefit per household, among

8.   Ibid.

9.   Esa Eslami, *Trends in Supplemental Nutrition Assistance Program Participation Rates: Fiscal Year 2010 to Fiscal Year 2012* (prepared by Mathematica Policy Research for the Department of Agriculture, July 2014), http://go.usa.gov/3xVbQ.

10. CBO placed households into 10 income groups of equal size, or deciles, on the basis of their annual after-tax cash income, which excludes SNAP benefits and was adjusted for household size by dividing income by the FPL. After-tax cash income closely approximates the resources available to a household before it receives SNAP benefits. Not all people in the lowest income decile participate in SNAP. For example, some are ineligible for non-financial reasons (such as immigration status), and some eligible people choose not to participate.

households receiving benefits, averaged $271, or $4.25 per person per day.[11]

In addition, other programs use participation in SNAP as a way to determine eligibility. For instance, school-age children in households that receive SNAP benefits are eligible for free breakfasts and free lunches through the School Breakfast Program and the National School Lunch Program.

Households that receive benefits tend to increase their total spending on food.[12] In addition, SNAP benefits free up resources that households can use to purchase other items and services. Evidence suggests that food security—which is generally defined as having access to adequate food for active, healthy living—increases in households when they begin receiving benefits.[13] However, SNAP benefits also reduce some people's incentive to work or their willingness to ask for help from family members or informal community networks. Participation in SNAP may have other consequences, such as effects on recipients' health or nutrition, but evidence has so far been inconclusive.[14]

SNAP Spending and Participation

Between fiscal years 2007 and 2014, federal spending on SNAP and the number of people receiving SNAP benefits increased significantly (see Figures 2 and 3).[15] Adjusted to exclude the effects of inflation, outlays for SNAP nearly doubled between those years, from $39 billion to $76 billion. Most of that increase in spending stemmed from the increasing number of participants, and the remainder resulted from an increase in spending per participant.

In fiscal year 2014, 47 million people—about 1 in 7 residents of the United States—received SNAP benefits in an average month. That number represents a dramatic increase from the roughly 26 million people (or 1 in 11 residents) who received benefits in fiscal year 2007. A key reason for the increase was the deep recession from December 2007 to June 2009 and the subsequent slow recovery, which increased the number of people with income low enough to qualify for the program.[16] Other factors also played a role, although their relative importance is unclear.[17]

In CBO's March 2015 baseline projections, which generally reflect the assumption that current laws will remain

11. Kelsey Farson Gray, *Characteristics of Supplemental Nutrition Assistance Program Households: Fiscal Year 2013*, SNAP-14-CHAR (submitted by Mathematica Policy Research to the Department of Agriculture, Food and Nutrition Service, Office of Policy Support, December 2014), http://go.usa.gov/3aKHP.

12. Mary Kay Fox, William Hamilton, and Biing-Hwan Lin, eds., *Effects of Food Assistance and Nutrition Programs on Nutrition and Health: Volume 3, Literature Review*, Food Assistance and Nutrition Research Report 19-3 (Department of Agriculture, Economic Research Service, October 2004), http://go.usa.gov/3cyU5; and Hilary W. Hoynes and Diane Whitmore Schanzenbach, "Consumption Responses to In-Kind Transfers: Evidence From the Introduction of the Food Stamp Program," *American Economic Journal: Applied Economics*, vol. 1, no. 4 (October 2009), pp. 109–139, http://tinyurl.com/qdxm9e2.

13. Mark Nord and Anne Marie Golla, *Does SNAP Decrease Food Insecurity? Untangling the Self-Selection Effect*, Economic Research Report 85 (Department of Agriculture, October 2009), http://go.usa.gov/3cyEC.

14. For a discussion of the difficulties in assessing the effects of SNAP on recipients' health and nutrition and the evidence to date about those effects, see Marianne Bitler, "The Health and Nutrition Effects of SNAP: Selection Into the Program and a Review of the Literature on Its Effects," in Judith Bartfeld and others, eds., *SNAP Matters: How Food Stamps Affect Health and Well-Being* (Stanford University Press, forthcoming).

15. The federal government pays the full cost of SNAP benefits, though it reimburses about half of states' spending on administrative costs.

16. For further discussion of the causes of the sharp increase in SNAP enrollment, see Congressional Budget Office, *The Supplemental Nutrition Assistance Program* (April 2012), www.cbo.gov/publication/43173. For evidence that the economic downturn was a key factor, see Peter Ganong and Jeffrey B. Liebman, *The Decline, Rebound, and Further Rise in SNAP Enrollment: Disentangling Business Cycle Fluctuations and Policy Changes*, Working Paper 19363 (National Bureau of Economic Research, August 2013), www.nber.org/papers/w19363.

17. For a discussion of other factors that may have played a role, see the testimony of Douglas J. Besharov, Professor, University of Maryland School of Public Policy, before the House Committee on Agriculture (February 25, 2015), http://go.usa.gov/3aH8A (PDF, 459 KB). For analysis of the contributions of those factors to the increased participation in SNAP, including evidence that changes in state policy played a significant role, see Peter Ganong and Jeffrey B. Liebman, *The Decline, Rebound, and Further Rise in SNAP Enrollment: Disentangling Business Cycle Fluctuations and Policy Changes*, Working Paper 19363 (National Bureau of Economic Research, August 2013), www.nber.org/papers/w19363; and Casey B. Mulligan, *The Redistribution Recession: How Labor Market Distortions Contracted the Economy* (Oxford University Press, 2012), http://tinyurl.com/ma789jb.

Figure 2.

SNAP Spending

Billions of Dollars

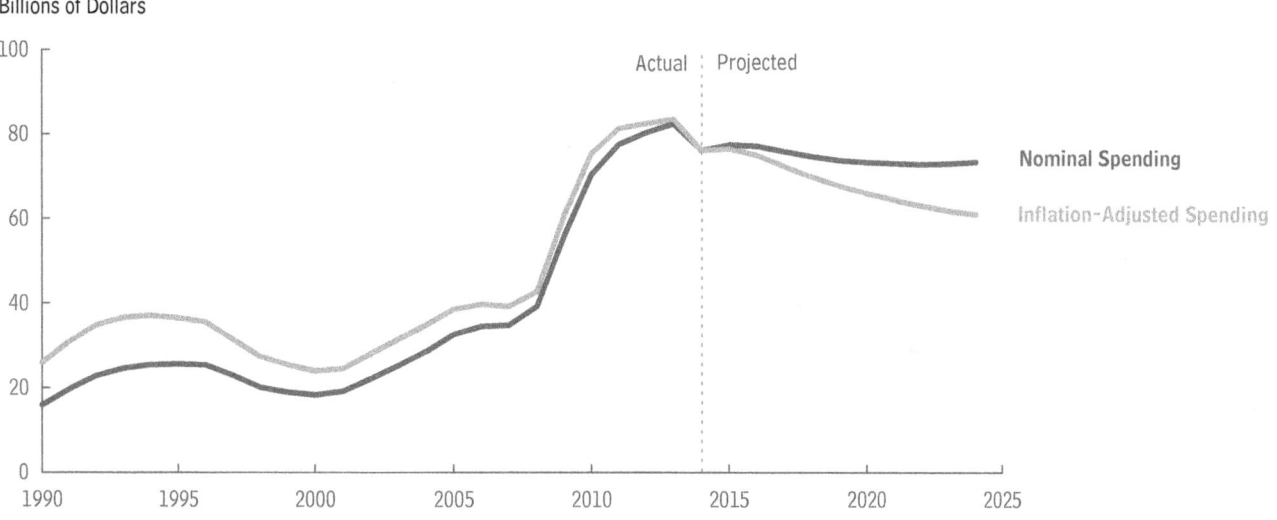

Source: Congressional Budget Office.

Notes: Data are annual. CBO's projections are from its March 2015 baseline.

   To adjust for inflation, CBO converted nominal dollars into fiscal year 2014 dollars, using the price index for personal consumption expenditures.

   SNAP = Supplemental Nutrition Assistance Program.

in place, inflation-adjusted spending on SNAP is projected to decline through fiscal year 2025, as is participation in the program.[18] Federal spending on SNAP in fiscal year 2025 is projected to be about $60 billion in 2014 dollars—about 20 percent less than it was in fiscal year 2014 but still about 50 percent more than it was in fiscal year 2007, before the recession and slow recovery. And roughly 33 million people—nearly 1 in 10 residents of the United States—are projected to receive SNAP benefits in fiscal year 2025. That would be about one-quarter more people than in fiscal year 2007 and a slightly larger share of the population.

Options to Reduce SNAP Spending

Some lawmakers have proposed reducing future spending on SNAP significantly. CBO therefore examined the effects on households' income of three policy options, each of which was designed to take full effect in 2016 and

to reduce federal spending on SNAP by 15 percent in that year:[19]

■ Reducing SNAP benefits for all participants by reducing the maximum benefit by 13 percent and leaving other program rules unchanged (which would result in benefit cuts for all beneficiaries);

■ Increasing the rate at which benefits decline from the maximum benefit, as a household's net income increases, from 30 percent of additional income to 49 percent; and

■ Reducing the gross income limit for eligibility from 130 percent to 67 percent of the FPL, while maintaining benefit amounts for those who remain eligible (including households with elderly or disabled members and households eligible because they receive cash assistance from certain other programs).

18. As the rules governing baseline projections specify, CBO's baseline projections for SNAP reflect the assumption that the program will be extended after it expires at the end of fiscal year 2018. Also, CBO reports its baseline projections in nominal dollars—that is, including the effects of inflation; the amounts reported in this report, however, have been adjusted to exclude the effects of inflation except where specified otherwise.

19. These options were chosen for illustrative purposes. Neither the size of the reduction nor the details of the options were designed to correspond to any particular legislative proposal. For the purposes of this report, CBO assumed that each option would be fully implemented by the beginning of fiscal year 2016; however, implementation could not, in fact, occur that quickly, so savings in the first year would be smaller.

Figure 3.

SNAP Participation and the Unemployment Rate

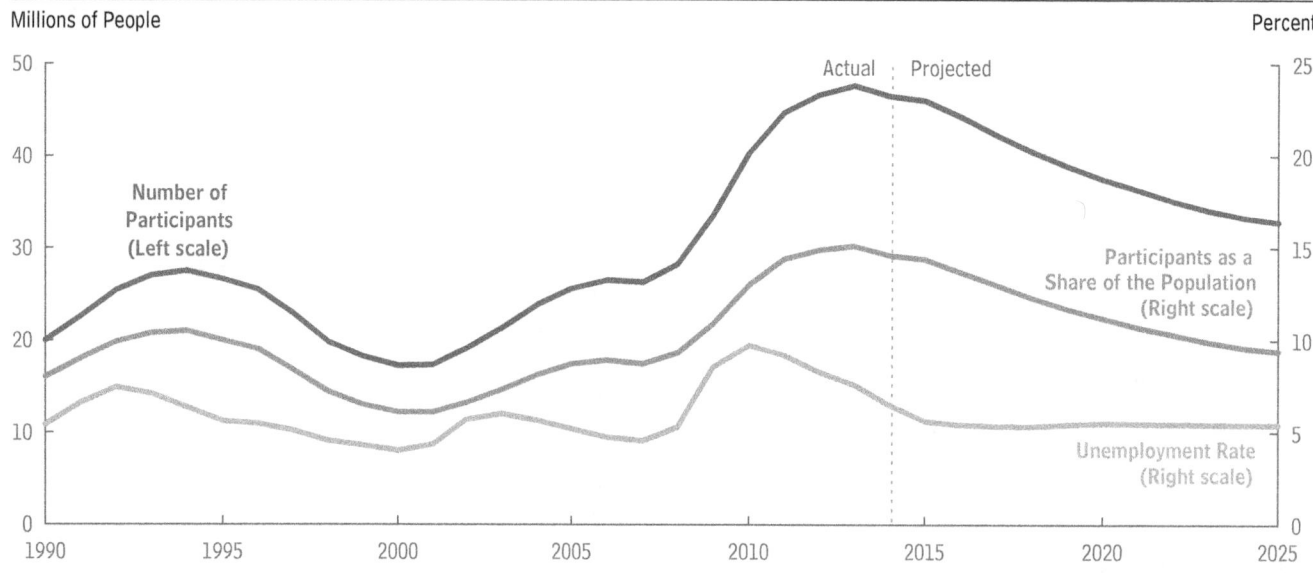

Millions of People

Percent

Source: Congressional Budget Office.

Notes: Data are annual. CBO's projections are from its March 2015 baseline.

SNAP = Supplemental Nutrition Assistance Program.

If policymakers wanted to use one of those approaches to cut spending by a different amount, the specifications of the options could be adjusted accordingly. For this report, CBO did not analyze the potential effects of another option that some policymakers have suggested: converting SNAP into a block grant program (see Box 1).[20]

Reducing Benefits for All Participants

In most years since 1996, the maximum SNAP benefit has been set at 100 percent of the cost of the Thrifty Food Plan.[21] Policymakers could reduce it to 87 percent

---

20. CBO has elsewhere examined a version of that option that would result in more savings than the options discussed here would. CBO has also examined an option that would reduce the gross income limit to 100 percent of the FPL—a smaller reduction than the one described in the third option here—and result in smaller savings than that third option would. For both of those options, see Congressional Budget Office, *Options for Reducing the Deficit: 2015 to 2024* (November 2014), pp. 10–11, www.cbo.gov/budget-options/2014. Other approaches that would save less than the options examined here include eliminating broad-based categorical eligibility and implementing a work requirement stricter than the one that currently exists for SNAP participants without dependents who are able to work.

of the cost of the TFP to reduce spending on the program by 15 percent in 2016, CBO estimates.[22] Provided that other benefit-calculation rules remained unchanged, most households that continued to receive benefits would see their benefits reduced by the same dollar amount by which the maximum benefit was reduced, and some households that would otherwise have been eligible for a small benefit would no longer be eligible for any benefit. In the range over which benefits declined as income increased (the part of the solid line that slopes downward in the top panel of Figure 4), each additional dollar of net income would still, as under current law, reduce a household's benefits by 30 cents.

---

21. The American Recovery and Reinvestment Act of 2009 temporarily increased benefits, beginning in April 2009; subsequent legislation eliminated that increase as of October 31, 2013.

22. A 13 percent reduction in the maximum benefit that left other program rules unchanged would result in a 15 percent reduction in spending on SNAP because it would reduce most benefits by the same number of dollars, which would translate into a larger percentage decline in the (smaller) benefits received by people in higher income groups.

Box 1.

The Implications of Converting SNAP Into a Block Grant Program

In the past, some policymakers have called for converting the Supplemental Nutrition Assistance Program (SNAP) into a block grant program. In such a program, the federal government would allocate set amounts—block grants—to the states.[1] That approach would probably give states more control over spending decisions and could, depending on the size of the block grants, either increase or decrease federal spending. But the effects of such a change on households' income would depend on the size of the block grants and on the conditions attached to them—as well as on decisions made by state governments, which are very difficult to predict. The effects would also depend on the extent to which the size of the block grants was linked to economic conditions.

Federal block grants generally afford state governments substantial control over spending decisions. In converting SNAP into a block grant program, policymakers could use that model and transfer much of the decisionmaking power from the federal government to the states—making SNAP more similar to Temporary Assistance for Needy Families, for instance.[2] Given such authority, states might be able to define eligibility and administer benefits in ways that better served their populations. Moreover, allowing states more flexibility in operating SNAP would result in more experimentation, and approaches that were successful in some states could be adopted by others. However, such flexibility might also let states spend funds in ways that federal policymakers would not have chosen. In addition, if the federal government did not require the block grants to be used exclusively on the SNAP program, state governments might use them to pay for other programs and reduce their own spending on those programs.

The effects of a block grant program on households' income are highly uncertain. Under block grant proposals that would reduce federal spending on SNAP by about 15 percent, as the options examined in this report would, average benefits paid by states would be significantly lower than the amounts projected under current law unless state or private sources made up some or all of the difference. Which recipients were affected by that cut in spending and how they were affected would depend on how states restructured their programs and how nonfederal spending changed. For instance, some states might reduce the maximum benefit, as in the first option analyzed here, while others might increase the benefit phaseout rate or reduce the gross income limit for eligibility, as in the second and third options. But a 15 percent cut in federal spending would probably eliminate benefits for some people who would otherwise have received them, significantly reduce the benefits of some people who remained in the program, or both.

The effects of a block grant program on households' income would also depend on whether the size of the grant depended on changes in economic conditions. For example, policymakers could decide to fix the size of the block grant in nominal dollars or to index it to inflation, allowing it to increase over time. Such structures would make spending by the federal government more predictable. Alternatively, policymakers could tie the size of the block grant to economic conditions, so that it increased during economic downturns and subsequent recoveries and decreased when the economy was relatively strong. Those automatic changes in spending would help stabilize the economy, reducing the depth of recessions. Furthermore, they would help prevent a situation in which, during a future economic downturn, an increase in the number of people eligible for benefits encouraged states (probably at a time when their own revenues were declining) to reduce the benefits received by each participant or to tighten eligibility, perhaps adding to people's hardship just when their own resources were reduced.

---

1. See Congressional Budget Office, *Federal Grants to State and Local Governments* (March 2013), www.cbo.gov/publication/43967.

2. See Congressional Budget Office, *Temporary Assistance for Needy Families: Spending and Policy Options* (January 2015), www.cbo.gov/publication/49887.

Figure 4.

Monthly Benefit for a Three-Person Household Under Three Options to Reduce SNAP Spending, 2016

Dollars

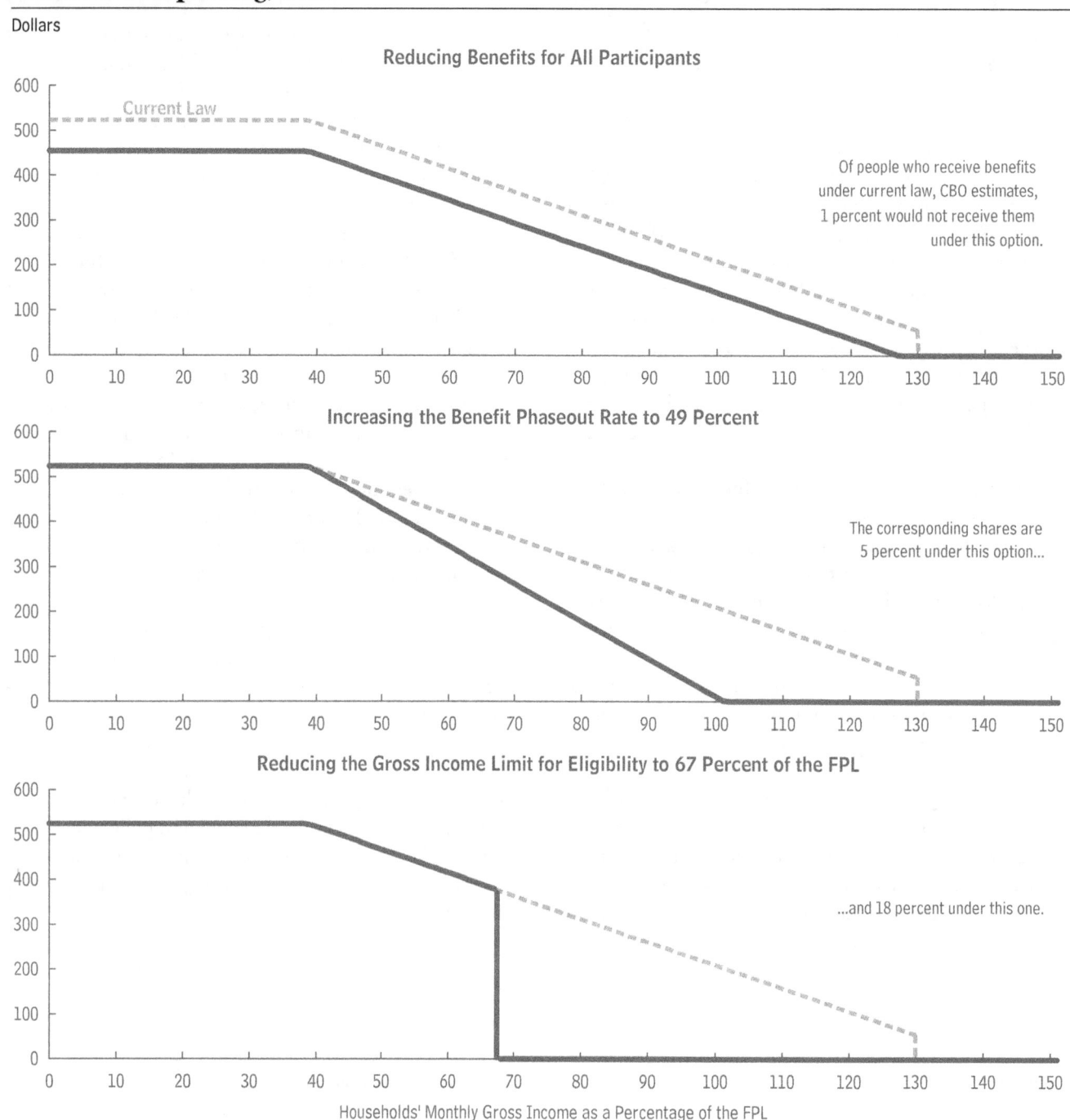

Source: Congressional Budget Office.

Notes: These benefits are for a three-person household that claims the maximum shelter deduction and is eligible for SNAP because it meets certain monthly income and asset requirements.

Gross income includes most cash income (such as earnings, Social Security benefits, Supplemental Security Income, and TANF assistance) and excludes most noncash income and in-kind benefits. It is a measure of income used to determine eligibility for SNAP.

FPL = federal poverty level (officially called the federal poverty guidelines); SNAP = Supplemental Nutrition Assistance Program.

Increasing the Benefit Phaseout Rate

Lawmakers could also reduce spending for SNAP by leaving the maximum benefit unchanged but increasing the rate at which benefits decline as households' net income increases. Increasing that rate from 30 percent of additional net income to 49 percent would reduce spending on SNAP by 15 percent in 2016, CBO estimates. (The higher rate is indicated by the steepness of the downward-sloping solid line in the middle panel of Figure 4.)

Reducing the Gross Income Limit

Under current law, a household that is not eligible for benefits through participation in certain programs and does not include an elderly or disabled member must have gross income no higher than 130 percent of the FPL to be eligible for SNAP. Lowering that gross income limit to 67 percent of the FPL while maintaining benefit amounts for those who remained eligible would reduce spending on SNAP by 15 percent in 2016, CBO estimates. In making that estimate, CBO assumed that the states currently using broad-based categorical eligibility and, consequently, a gross income limit that is effectively higher than 130 percent of the FPL would be required to use the new 67 percent limit for all households except those that included elderly or disabled members or that received cash assistance from other programs.

As under current law, benefits would decline by 30 cents for every $1 increase in net income in the range over which benefits declined as income increased. However, a much larger loss in benefits would result when income rose one dollar above the new eligibility limit. (For example, in the illustrative case shown in the bottom panel of Figure 4, benefits would decline by about $375 per month at that point.)

CBO's Analytical Approach

For its analysis, CBO simulated the effects of the options described above on the SNAP benefits received by households in various groups and thus on their income. (For additional information about that simulation, see the appendix.) CBO also considered how the options would affect people's incentives to work, but the agency did not incorporate any changes in labor earnings into its estimates of the effects of the policy options on income.

CBO focused on after-tax cash income—that is, market income and cash transfers, net of federal taxes paid or refundable tax credits received—plus SNAP benefits during calendar year 2016. Market income in this analysis consists of cash wages and salaries; business income; capital gains (that is, profits realized from the sale of assets); capital income, excluding capital gains; income received in retirement for past services; and income from certain other sources. Cash transfers include payments of benefits from Social Security, unemployment insurance, SSI, TANF, veterans' programs, workers' compensation, and state and local government assistance programs. Federal taxes incorporated in this analysis include individual income taxes and payroll (or social insurance) taxes. Health-related benefits, such as employment-based health insurance, Medicare, Medicaid, and the value of subsidies provided through federal health insurance exchanges, are not included in CBO's measure of after-tax cash income.[23] For most of the households considered in this analysis, adding market income to cash transfers yields a result that is similar to the gross income that SNAP uses to determine eligibility, except that the basis is annual instead of monthly.

The Effects of Reducing SNAP Benefits on Households With Different Amounts of Income

Each of the three options described above would reduce spending on SNAP by 15 percent, or $11.5 billion, in 2016. But who would be affected and by how much differ from option to option. The first option would have larger effects on households with after-tax income (excluding SNAP benefits) in the lowest 10 percent (or lowest decile) of the income distribution than would the other two options; those other options would have the largest effects on households in the second decile of the income distribution, according to most measures. Households in a given decile of annual after-tax cash income would be affected similarly, on average, by the second option and by the third (despite the differences suggested

---

23. For additional information about the components of after-tax cash income, see Congressional Budget Office, *The Distribution of Household Income and Federal Taxes, 2011* (November 2014), www.cbo.gov/publication/49440. That report's definition of after-tax income also included several forms of labor income other than cash wages and salaries, as well as in-kind benefits other than those provided by SNAP (such as those provided by Medicaid), and it accounted for federal excise taxes.

Figure 5.

The Effects on Total SNAP Benefits in 2016 of Three Options to Reduce SNAP Spending by 15 Percent

The total reduction in spending would be $11.5 billion for each option.

Billions of 2016 Dollars

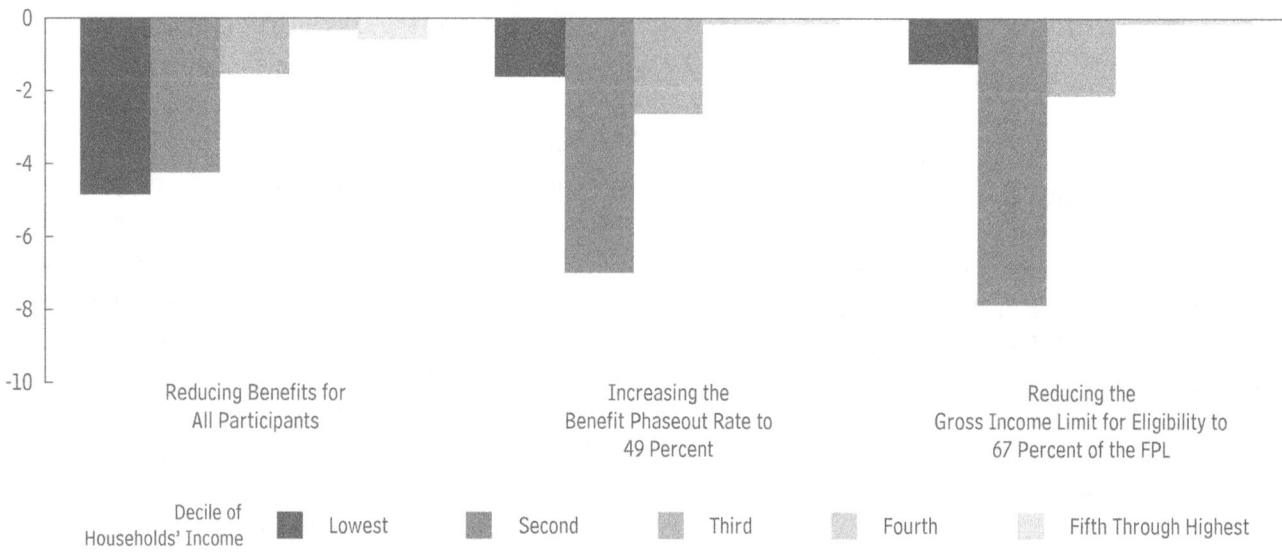

Source: Congressional Budget Office.

Notes: CBO placed households into 10 income groups of equal size, or deciles, on the basis of their annual after-tax cash income, which excludes SNAP benefits and was adjusted for household size by dividing income by the FPL. After-tax cash income consists of market income and cash transfers, net of federal taxes paid or refundable tax credits received.

In 2016, CBO estimates, three-person households in the lowest decile of the income distribution will have annual after-tax cash income below about $15,000, those in the second decile will have income between about $15,000 and $25,000, and those in the third decile will have income between about $25,000 and $32,000.

FPL = federal poverty level (officially called the federal poverty guidelines); SNAP = Supplemental Nutrition Assistance Program.

by Figure 4, which ranks households by monthly gross income).[24] Although the options would affect people's incentives to work, CBO did not incorporate those effects into its estimates of how much the options would affect the federal budget and households' income.

The Effects of Reducing Benefits for All Participants

If the maximum SNAP benefit was reduced by 13 percent and other program rules were left unchanged (which would result in benefit cuts for all beneficiaries), as the first option specifies, about 1 percent of the households that would receive SNAP benefits under current law

would no longer receive them. CBO estimated the following effects on households in various income groups in 2016:

■ The benefits of households with income in the lowest decile of the income distribution would fall by about $5 billion (see Figure 5). That decline would equal about $600 for the year, on average, for each household that would receive benefits under current law (see the top panel of Figure 6 on page 14). Among all households in that income group—including not only those that would receive benefits under current law, but also those that would not and would therefore experience no decline in income—the option would reduce income for the year by about 4 percent, on average (see the bottom panel of Figure 7 on page 15).[25]

---

24. The reason is that each decile of annual after-tax income includes households with a broad range of monthly gross income, some of which would be affected more by the second option and some of which would be affected more by the third.

■ For households with income in the second decile of the income distribution, benefits would fall by about $4 billion. For households that would receive benefits under current law, average benefits would fall by about $550 for the year; among all households in that income group, average income for the year would decline by 1½ percent.

■ The benefits of households with income in the third decile of the income distribution would decline by a smaller amount—less than $2 billion. However, because households in that decile tend to be larger and thus receive larger benefits, the average decline in benefits per household would be larger—about $700 for the year. Among all households in that income group, average income for the year would decline by roughly one-half of one percent.

■ The reduction in benefits for households in the higher income deciles would be smaller still—about $1 billion in total. For the relatively small number of households in those groups that would receive benefits under current law, the average loss in benefits would range between $500 and $600 for the year, and for all households in those groups, income for the year would decline by less than one-tenth of one percent, on average.

Among the households receiving SNAP benefits, those with the lowest income—which might place the highest value on those benefits—would thus see an average reduction in benefits that was similar, in dollar terms, to the reduction experienced by recipients with higher income.

The Effects of Increasing the Benefit Phaseout Rate

If the benefit phaseout rate was raised from 30 percent to 49 percent and the maximum benefit remained unchanged, as the second option specifies, about 5 percent of the households that would receive SNAP benefits under current law would no longer receive them. CBO estimated the following effects on households in various income groups in 2016:

■ Benefits would decline by about $1.5 billion for households with income in the lowest decile of the income distribution. That figure is much smaller than the corresponding one for the first option because

most of the households in that group that received SNAP benefits would receive the maximum benefit and would therefore be unaffected by this option. Households that would receive benefits under current law would see a decline in their benefits of about $200 over the course of the year, on average. For all households in that group, income for the year would fall by about 1½ percent, on average.

■ Households with income in the second decile of the income distribution would see the largest total decline in benefits—about $7 billion, accounting for about 60 percent of the federal budgetary savings. The average benefit for households that would receive benefits under current law would fall by about $900 for the year. That decline is much larger than the decline for households in the lowest decile because this option reduces benefits only for people with positive net income—who are likelier to be in the second decile than in the lowest decile. Average income for all households in the second decile would decline by about 2½ percent for the year.

■ Households with income in the third decile of the income distribution would lose about $2.5 billion in benefits. The average benefit for households that would receive benefits under current law would fall by about $1,200 for the year—even more than for households in the second decile, because households in the third decile generally have higher net income and thus would be subject to a larger decline in benefits. Average income for all households in the third decile would decline by less than 1 percent for the year; that decline is much smaller than for households in the second decile because fewer households in this group receive SNAP benefits and because the benefits generally represent a smaller share of their income.

■ The reduction in benefits for the groups with higher income would be less than $0.5 billion. Among households that would receive benefits under current law, benefits would decline by between $100 and $300 for the year, on average. Those reductions are smaller than under the first option because households with income in the fourth decile and above would be likelier to have members who worked for only part of the year, had no income in other months, and so received the maximum SNAP benefit (which this option would not reduce) for part of the year. For all households in those groups, income for the year would decline by less than one-tenth of one percent, on average.

---

25. As this report notes above, not all people in the lowest income decile participate in SNAP. For example, some are ineligible for nonfinancial reasons (such as immigration status), and some eligible people choose not to participate.

Figure 6.

The Average Effects on Households Receiving Benefits in 2016 of Three Options to Reduce SNAP Spending by 15 Percent

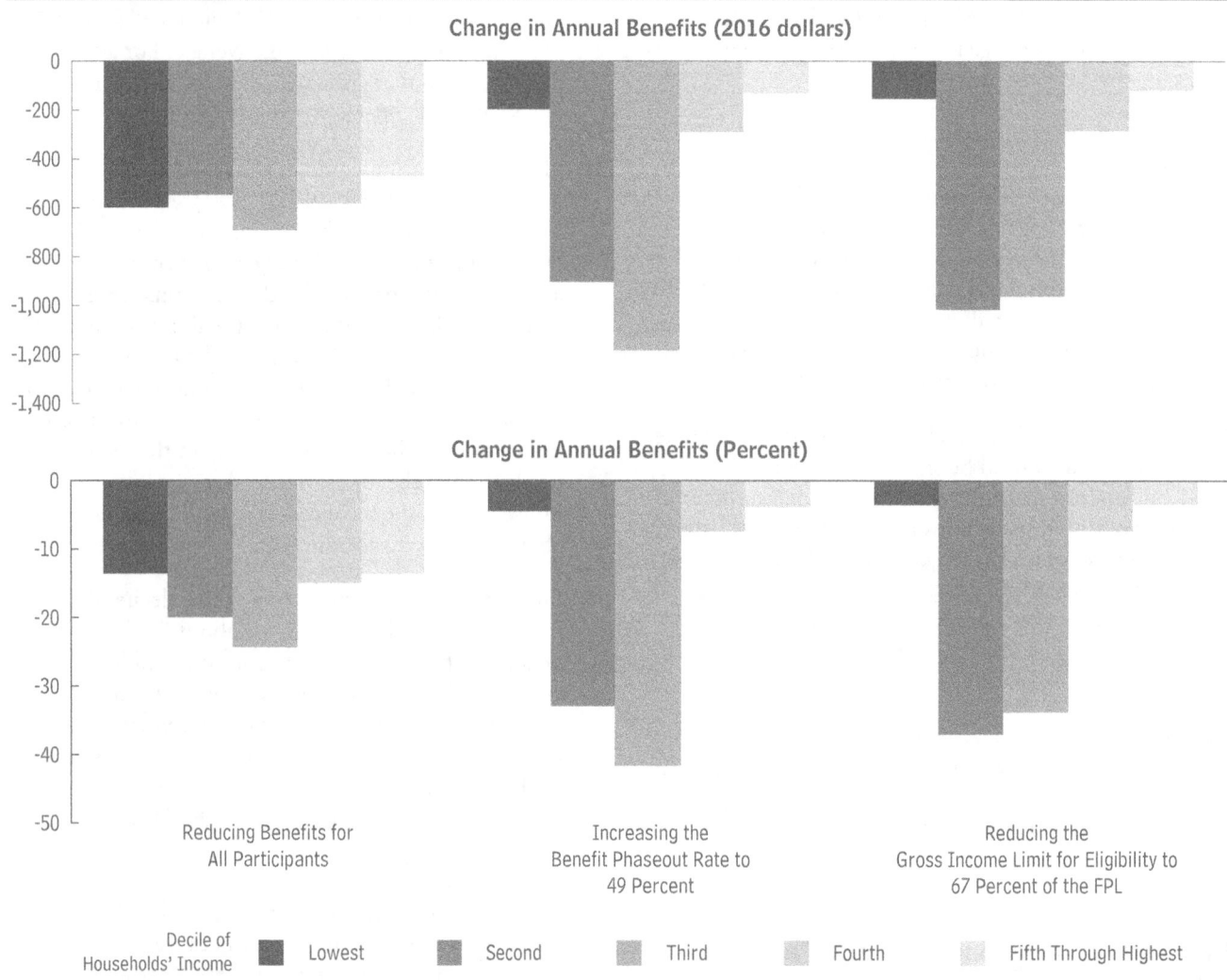

Source: Congressional Budget Office.

Notes: Effects are shown only for households that would receive SNAP benefits.

CBO placed households into 10 income groups of equal size, or deciles, on the basis of their annual after-tax cash income, which excludes SNAP benefits and was adjusted for household size by dividing income by the FPL. After-tax cash income consists of market income and cash transfers, net of federal taxes paid or refundable tax credits received.

The dollar change in annual benefits was calculated by dividing the total change in benefits by the average number of households receiving benefits each month. The Food and Nutrition Service estimates that the number of households that receive benefits at some point in the year is 30 percent larger than the average number of households receiving benefits each month.

In 2016, CBO estimates, three-person households in the lowest decile of the income distribution will have annual after-tax cash income below about $15,000, those in the second decile will have income between about $15,000 and $25,000, and those in the third decile will have income between about $25,000 and $32,000.

FPL = federal poverty level (officially called the federal poverty guidelines); SNAP = Supplemental Nutrition Assistance Program.

Figure 7.

The Average Effects on All Households in 2016 of Three Options to Reduce SNAP Spending by 15 Percent

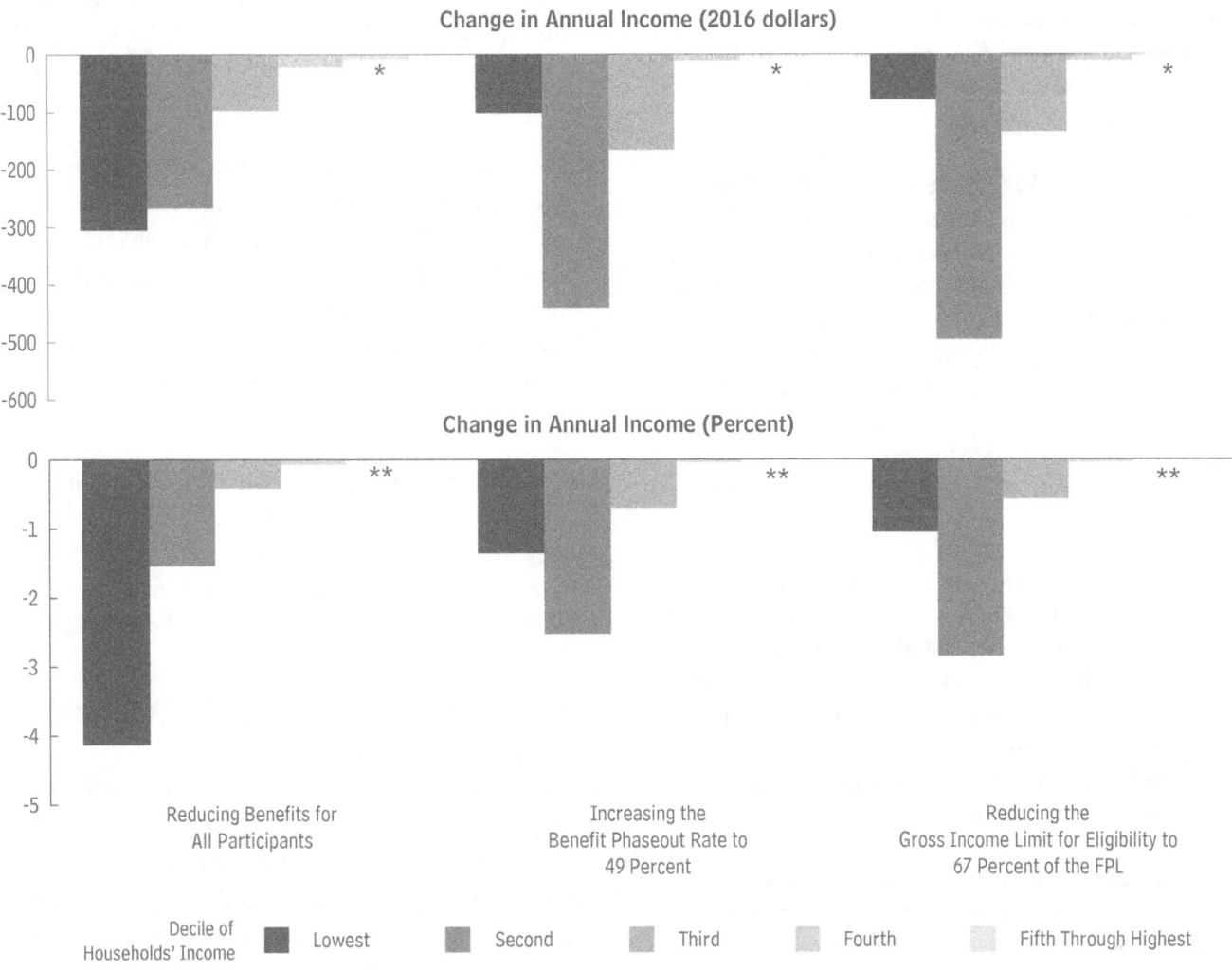

Source: Congressional Budget Office.

Notes: Effects are shown for all households, including those that would not receive SNAP benefits.

CBO placed households into 10 income groups of equal size, or deciles, on the basis of their annual after-tax cash income, which excludes SNAP benefits and was adjusted for household size by dividing income by the FPL. However, the effects shown on the households' income are effects on after-tax income plus SNAP benefits. After-tax cash income consists of market income and cash transfers, net of federal taxes paid or refundable tax credits received.

In 2016, CBO estimates, three-person households in the lowest decile of the income distribution will have annual after-tax cash income below about $15,000, those in the second decile will have income between about $15,000 and $25,000, and those in the third decile will have income between about $25,000 and $32,000.

FPL = federal poverty level (officially called the federal poverty guidelines); SNAP = Supplemental Nutrition Assistance Program; * = between zero and -$10; ** = between zero and -0.01 percent.

Under this option, a household receiving SNAP benefits and with income in the range in which benefits are being phased out would need to devote 49 cents of each additional dollar of net income to food purchases, rather than the current 30 cents (if it wanted to obtain the same amount of food). That share is more than most unassisted households spend on food from each additional dollar that they earn, in CBO's assessment.[26]

The Effects of Reducing the Gross Income Limit

If households with income above 67 percent of the FPL were no longer eligible for SNAP, but benefits were maintained for those who remained eligible (including households with elderly or disabled members and households eligible because they received cash assistance from certain other programs), as the third option specifies, 18 percent of the households that would receive benefits under current law would not receive them. CBO estimated the following effects on households in various income groups in 2016:

■ Households with income in the lowest decile would not be affected much; their total benefits would fall by just over $1 billion. Among the households that would receive benefits under current law, benefits over the year would decline by about $150, on average. Among all households in the lowest decile of the income distribution, income for the year would decline by about 1 percent, on average.

■ Households with income in the second decile of the income distribution would see the largest total reduction in benefits—nearly $8 billion, accounting for about two-thirds of the federal budgetary savings. The average benefit for the households in that group that would receive benefits under current law would fall by about $1,000 over the year. That decline is much larger than the decline for households in the lowest decile because this option, like the second one, reduces benefits only for people who have positive net income, and those people are likelier to be in the second decile than in the lowest. Average income for all households in the second decile would decline by about 3 percent for the year.

■ Households with income in the third decile of the income distribution would lose about $2 billion in benefits. The average benefit for households that would receive benefits under current law would fall by about $1,000 for the year, and average income for all households in the third decile would decline by about one-half of one percent.

■ For households in the groups with higher income, the overall decline in benefits would be less than $0.5 billion. For the households that would receive benefits under current law, benefits would decline by between $100 and $300 over the year, on average. For all households in those income groups, income for the year would decline by less than one-tenth of one percent, on average.

Under this option, the difference in after-tax cash income between households that received substantial benefits and those that received none could be as small as one dollar. As a result, even a slight increase in such income would result in a sharp cut in benefits for some households.

The Effects of Reducing SNAP Benefits on Labor Income

In cases in which the government provides a benefit that gradually declines as recipients' earnings rise, eliminating the benefit for everyone would generally increase the amount of work performed by former recipients. That effect would occur for two reasons. First, because there would be no offsetting decline in benefits associated with an increase in income, the after-tax compensation for an additional hour of work would increase, making work more valuable relative to other uses of a person's time. Second, because the benefits would be eliminated, people's total after-tax income for any given amount of work would be lower, diminishing their standard of living unless they worked more hours.[27]

The options examined in this report, however, eliminate benefits only for some recipients and either maintain or reduce them for others. Depending on its details, that sort of change can encourage some people to work more but discourage others from doing so. CBO assessed those effects, although the agency did not quantify their impact on labor income.

---

26. For a discussion of the share of income spent on food by households with different amounts of income, see Department of Agriculture, Economic Research Service, "Food Spending as a Share of Income Declines as Income Rises" (November 25, 2014), http://go.usa.gov/3CqdR.

Under the first option, the rate at which most recipients' benefits fell as they worked more would not change, so their compensation for an additional hour of work would be unaltered. However, because the option would reduce benefits for all recipients, those who were healthy enough would tend to work more in order to partially offset the decline in their standard of living. In light of the empirical evidence about the responsiveness of the supply of labor to changes in tax rates, CBO expects that the additional labor income that would be earned under this option would probably offset only a small fraction of the benefits lost.[28] The additional earnings would also increase the federal government's budgetary savings by a small percentage by boosting tax revenues and reducing

spending on SNAP and other forms of government assistance; that effect would be small, partly because the hourly wages of the affected people would generally be low.

Under the second and third options, benefits would not change for households with no net income, but some workers in households with net income would see their benefits diminished more quickly as they worked more— lowering both their after-tax compensation from each hour of work and their total after-tax income from a given amount of work. That quicker decline would tend to discourage additional work, on net, for those people. Further, the second and third options would eliminate some people's benefits at their existing income levels, which might encourage them either to work less (in order to resume getting benefits) or to work more (for the same two reasons that eliminating a benefit for all recipients tends to increase work). On net, CBO expects that the second and third options would reduce labor income. That reduction in earnings would probably be only a small fraction of the reduction in benefits, in CBO's assessment, and it would decrease the budgetary savings by a small percentage by slightly reducing tax revenues and increasing spending on SNAP and other forms of government assistance.

27. Researchers have found that after the Food Stamp program was introduced, the number of hours worked over the course of a year among families headed by a single woman fell significantly. See Hilary Williamson Hoynes and Diane Whitmore Schanzenbach, "Work Incentives and the Food Stamp Program," *Journal of Public Economics*, vol. 96, nos. 1–2 (February 2012), pp. 151–162, http://dx.doi.org/10.1016/j.jpubeco.2011.08.006. For further discussion of the work disincentives created by public assistance programs, see Casey B. Mulligan, *The Redistribution Recession: How Labor Market Distortions Contracted the Economy* (Oxford University Press, 2012), http://tinyurl.com/ma789jb.

28. Congressional Budget Office, *How the Supply of Labor Responds to Changes in Fiscal Policy* (October 2012), www.cbo.gov/publication/43674.

Appendix:
The Basis of CBO's Analysis

This appendix describes the steps that the Congressional Budget Office took to arrive at the estimates in this report:

- Obtaining historical data on households' annual income for a representative sample of the population;

- Using those historical data to project households' income in 2016;

- Using those projections to estimate the eligibility of each household for the Supplemental Nutrition Assistance Program (SNAP) in 2016;

- Estimating the probability of participation in SNAP for each of the eligible households, as well as the size of the SNAP benefits that participating households would receive in 2016 under current law; and

- Estimating the effects of the options discussed in this report on those benefits and on households' income.

Historical Data on Households' Income

Information on households' income for this analysis came from two main sources: the Internal Revenue Service's Statistics of Income (SOI) and the Census Bureau's Current Population Survey (CPS). The core data, which came from the SOI, consisted of about 160,000 individual income tax returns that together constitute a nationally representative sample of tax returns. CBO supplemented those data with data from the CPS—specifically, with data from the CPS's Annual Social and Economic Supplement, which include demographic characteristics and income for about 70,000 households that are likewise a nationally representative sample.

The SOI and CPS data were for income in calendar year 2006. Because CBO faced time constraints in producing this analysis, and because the agency had used the 2006 data in previous work on SNAP, it again used those data to conduct this analysis. The 2006 data have another advantage over data from the most recent year available, 2011: They were not affected by the 2007–2009 recession and subsequent slow recovery, so the distribution of income that they describe may be more representative of the distribution of income that will exist in 2016.

Both the SOI and the CPS lack important information needed for estimating and comparing households' after-tax income over time. The SOI does not include information about people who do not file federal tax returns, and it does not report all income from government cash transfer programs. It also offers no information on the receipt of in-kind transfers and benefits, and it is organized by tax-filing units rather than by households. The CPS lacks detailed information on high-income households, it does not report capital gains, it underreports other income from capital, and it lacks information on the deductions and adjustments necessary to compute taxes.

Together, however, the two sources can provide a more comprehensive picture. To overcome limitations in each source of data, CBO organized CPS records into tax-filing units and then statistically matched each SOI record to a corresponding CPS record on the basis of demographic characteristics and income. Each pairing resulted in a new record, to which CBO assigned the demographic characteristics of the CPS record and the income reported in the SOI. (Some types of income—certain transfers and in-kind benefits, for example—appear only in the CPS; their values in the new record were drawn directly from that survey.) Because some households are not required to file tax returns, the SOI is not representative of every household in the nation. To create a sample that *was* representative of the entire population, once all of the SOI tax-filing units were matched to corresponding CPS tax-filing units, CBO recorded the remaining CPS records as non-tax-filing units, and their income values were taken directly from the CPS. The resulting sample was a combination of records from the SOI and the CPS.

The SOI and CPS data have several advantages over the administrative data in the SNAP Quality Control database, which the government uses to assess the accuracy of eligibility determinations and benefit calculations. First, the SOI and the CPS cover the full population, not just SNAP recipients, allowing an evaluation of the effects of policy changes on the population as a whole. Second, the SOI and CPS data provide a more comprehensive measure of households' income, as well as an annual, rather than a monthly, estimate of that income. Third, because CBO regularly makes projections about the future using the SOI and the CPS, it has developed methods for doing so; using the SNAP Quality Control database in the analysis of the distribution of income would have required CBO to develop new methods.

Households' Income in 2016

Because this analysis estimates the effects of policy changes that would occur in 2016, CBO made various adjustments to the 2006 sample just described so that it would accord with CBO's projection of the characteristics of the population in 2016. That process involved adjusting the weighting of the sample to account for expected changes in the composition of the population and in employment levels. CBO then increased the amounts of different types of income in each record to levels projected for 2016. Wages, interest, and dividends were adjusted to be consistent with CBO's macroeconomic projections; Social Security and unemployment insurance benefits, to match CBO's spending projections for those programs; and capital gains and retirement income, to be consistent with amounts underlying CBO's revenue projections. The resulting sample should therefore be representative of U.S. households in 2016, as long as the underlying demographic and economic projections are accurate.

Eligibility for SNAP in 2016

SNAP benefits are awarded to so-called food assistance units, which are groups of people who live together—no family relationship is required—and share the purchase, preparation, and consumption of food. Although food assistance units can be smaller than households, they are often equivalent and are referred to as households in this analysis. (The tax-filing units used as the basis for some of the income data in this analysis are also generally the same size as or smaller than households.)

CBO applied SNAP's rules to estimate whether each household in its sample would be eligible for the program. A household may become eligible for SNAP by participating in other programs or by demonstrating sufficiently low income and assets. Although participation in other programs is currently the most common way that households become eligible, almost all SNAP benefits are paid to households whose gross monthly income, net monthly income, and assets are, in fact, below the required thresholds.

Eligibility by Participating in Other Programs

To determine whether a household would be eligible for SNAP because it received cash assistance from Temporary Assistance for Needy Families (TANF) or Supplemental Security Income (SSI), CBO used data on the receipt of cash assistance from those programs. All recipients of cash assistance from TANF or SSI were considered eligible for SNAP.

A household can also be eligible for SNAP if it receives noncash benefits from TANF, but CBO did not have data about the recipients of those benefits in its combination of SOI and CPS records. Instead, CBO assumed that in states that extend eligibility to recipients of noncash TANF benefits, the higher income and asset thresholds associated with that eligibility applied to all people in those states. CBO's approach to estimating participation in SNAP accounted for all households that would be eligible because they participated in other programs, as this appendix explains below.

Eligibility by Demonstrating Low Income and Few Assets

To determine whether each household in its 2016 sample would meet the monthly gross income requirement, CBO started with annual data on that household's market income and cash transfers and made certain adjustments to correspond to the definition of gross income used by SNAP. Next, CBO estimated the number of weeks that each household worked during the year to project the number of months in which the household had earned income. The earned income was allocated equally among all months in which the household worked. Unearned income, by contrast, was allocated equally among all 12 months of the year. A household met the requirement for eligibility in a particular month if its gross income in that month was below 130 percent of the federal poverty guideline. (A household with an elderly person or a person who was receiving disability payments of certain types was considered exempt from that requirement, as SNAP allows.)

To determine whether a household would meet the monthly net income requirement, CBO started with its estimate of the household's monthly gross income and incorporated five deductions allowed by SNAP: a standard deduction for all households and deductions related to earnings, housing costs, dependent care, and medical expenses. Information about housing costs was derived from data on similar households in the Census Bureau's American Community Survey. A household met the monthly net income requirement in a particular month if its net income was below 100 percent of the federal poverty guideline.

To determine whether a household would meet the asset requirement, CBO estimated that household's assets, using data on the household's capital income from assets of certain types and estimates of how much income would typically be provided per dollar of asset value by an asset of each type. That approach probably underestimates assets. However, other data indicate that few households meeting the gross and net income requirements have enough assets of the types that are counted in the asset requirement—such as cash, money in checking accounts, stocks, and bonds—to exceed the allowed amounts, which are a few thousand dollars and depend on whether at least one person in a household is at least 60 years old. Certain other assets that a household may own, such as a primary residence, a vehicle (in most states), and money in retirement or education savings accounts, are not counted in the asset requirement.

Participation in SNAP and Benefit Amounts in 2016

CBO used a combination of approaches to project the probability of each household's participation in SNAP in 2016. First, CBO used the estimate of the total number of participants in 2016 that was prepared as part of the agency's March 2015 baseline budget projections.[1] That estimate is based on the program's eligibility criteria, trends in overall program participation rates, CBO's forecast of unemployment rates, and other factors. In this analysis, CBO set the *overall* participation rate for 2016 so that, when multiplied by the number of households that are estimated to be eligible in that year, it would equal the number of households projected to receive SNAP benefits in CBO's baseline.

However, the participation rates for some groups (as defined by households' characteristics, such as income and size) are higher or lower than that overall rate. To see how participation rates have varied among such groups in the past, CBO estimated group-specific rates for each year from 2006 to 2011, using detailed administrative data on participants and its own estimates of the number of eligible households. (Because the historical participation rates were based on the actual number of participants in SNAP, CBO's approach in this step accounted not only for participants who demonstrated sufficiently low income and few assets but also for all participants who became eligible by participating in other programs—including those who received only noncash TANF benefits.) CBO then used those group-specific rates to deduce each group's average representation among all SNAP participants during those years. Finally, CBO projected a total set of eligible households in 2016 in which each group was represented to the same extent that it was, on average, from 2006 to 2011. For example, households with extremely low income have historically represented a high proportion of all SNAP participants, and they represent the same high proportion in CBO's projection for 2016.

CBO estimated the *potential* SNAP benefit for each eligible household by applying the rules of the program. (Those rules vary benefits according to households' size and monthly net income.) CBO then multiplied that

---

1. Congressional Budget Office, "Supplemental Nutrition Assistance Program—Baseline Projections" (March 2015), www.cbo.gov/publication/44211.

potential benefit by the participation rate of the household's group. To arrive at the total benefit amount, CBO followed that procedure for all eligible households, added the results together, and then adjusted the total amount of benefits received by each group by an equal percentage so that the overall total was aligned with CBO's baseline projection of benefits. That adjustment was equal to about 2 percent of total benefits in 2016.

Effects of the Options

For this analysis, CBO crafted options that would each reduce spending on SNAP by 15 percent, or $11.5 billion, in 2016, relative to the agency's baseline projection. CBO then estimated the effects of the options on the distribution of households' income.

To find policy specifications that would result in the $11.5 billion reduction, CBO used its standard techniques for estimating costs of proposals and varied the key parameters—such as the maximum benefit amount, the benefit reduction rate, and the gross income limit—until the specified amount was reached. Those estimates were based, in part, on data from the SNAP Quality Control database. However, those techniques did not account for the way each option might change the supply of labor and in turn affect the budget. Following the long-standing convention of not incorporating macroeconomic effects into cost estimates—a practice that has been followed in the Congressional budget process since it was established in 1974—CBO typically produces cost estimates that reflect the assumption that macroeconomic variables, such as gross domestic product and

employment, will remain fixed at the values that they are projected to reach under current law. (Earlier this year, the House of Representatives adopted a rule that requires CBO and the Joint Committee on Taxation to include the budgetary feedback of any macroeconomic effects in cost estimates for some major pieces of legislation; the effects on the deficit of the options examined here are about one-quarter of the amount that would trigger that requirement.)

To estimate the effects of the options on benefits received by households with different amounts of income, CBO estimated eligibility, participation, and benefit amounts for households under the specifications of each option. The agency then examined changes in the households' SNAP benefits and after-tax cash income relative to the amounts projected under current law. Although the options would affect people's incentives to work (as the report discusses), changes in the supply of labor were not incorporated into this part of the analysis either. In CBO's view, changes in income that result from reductions in benefits are different in character from changes in income that result from people's choices about whether to work more or less. For instance, if people receive $100 less in benefits per month and do not alter their work, they lose that income and gain nothing; by contrast, if they choose to work less and earn $100 less a month, they lose that income but gain time to do other things, so the total reduction in their well-being is not as great. CBO therefore did not combine the two types of change in this analysis.

List of Tables and Figures

About This Document

This Congressional Budget Office report was prepared at the request of Congressman Hoyer (the House Minority Whip) and Congresswoman Barbara Lee. In keeping with CBO's mandate to provide objective, impartial analysis, the report makes no recommendations.

Molly Dahl, Kathleen FitzGerald, Edward Harris, and Marvin Ward conducted the analysis and prepared the report, with guidance from Joseph Kile, Sam Papenfuss, and David Weiner and assistance from Tristan Hanon and Chung Kim. Linda Bilheimer and William Carrington provided helpful comments.

Randy Aussenberg of the Congressional Research Service, Karen Cunnyngham of Mathematica Policy Research, Dottie Rosenbaum of the Center on Budget and Policy Priorities, Rachel Sheffield of the Heritage Foundation, and James Ziliak of the University of Kentucky also offered useful comments. The assistance of external reviewers implies no responsibility for the final product, which rests solely with CBO.

Jeffrey Kling and Robert Sunshine reviewed the report, Benjamin Plotinsky edited it, and Maureen Costantino and Jeanine Rees prepared it for publication. An electronic version is available on CBO's website (www.cbo.gov/publication/49978).

Douglas W. Elmendorf
Director

March 2015

www.ingramcontent.com/pod-product-compliance
Lightning Source LLC
Chambersburg PA
CBHW080628180526
45168CB00007B/3092